GW00362926

OMNIUM GATHERUM
A TRANS-GENRE TRANS-GRENS ANTHOLOGY

* * *

EDITED BY SARA RICH

* * *

DRAGOMAN EDITING & PUBLISHING

LEUVEN – BELGIUM

ISBN: 978-9-08213-554-1
NUR: 309

Cover design: Sara Rich

Text body is set in Traditional Arabic; title headings are set in Castellar; and name subheadings are set in Adobe Caslon Pro.

Published in 2014 by
Dragoman Editing & Publishing
Alfons Roelandtsstraat 8, box 1
3010 Kessel-lo (Leuven)
Belgium

www.DragomanEditing.com
DragomanEditing@gmail.com

TABLE OF CONTENTS

FOREWORD

As an archaeologist, I am naturally drawn to assemblages. This also happens to be the artistic process that I use for creating three-dimensional works. Not surprisingly, then, as an editor, anthologies appeal to me as yet another form of assemblage: bringing together diverse components into a cohesive whole. One of the greatest privileges of this job is being surrounded by diverse young literary and visual storytellers from around the world. In this anthology, there is a gathering, less of miscellaneous stories, but more a diverse group of storytellers, who bring their craft with them to the proverbial table. These stories, like the individuals they represent, are imaginative and honest, frustrated and hopeful, lost and found. They describe something that everyone, without exception, can relate to: the experience of being (or feeling) strange.

How the contributors interpreted this sense of feeling or being was up to them. And beyond interpretation, each has also selected a different method of translation. Each work is trans-*genre*, trans-*grens*, challenging abstract categories and geographical borders to confront the oddity of the individual and contribute to the uniqueness of this diverse gathering. Collectively, we invite you to turn these pages and welcome you to join us in this *omnium gatherum*.

Sara Rich, Ph.D.
Leuven, Belgium
19 April 2014

DOUGLAS AND WINSTON

Callum Dawson

Douglas was a normal man. He had many normal things: he wore normal clothes, drove a normal car, had a normal job, and lived in a perfectly normal apartment building. He was completely normal from head to toe and proud to be so! He liked to go through his days without surprises, and he ended every day by sitting down to tea at half-past six without interruption. Some said Douglas ran like clockwork, and he planned every day by the tick-tock of his watch. He had no idea what he would do if things happened that he did not plan.

One day, Douglas arrived home from work as usual at five o'clock. He took off his normal hat, normal shoes, and normal tie, and sat down to watch TV. He started cooking dinner by six o'clock and had it hot and ready by six-thirty. He sat down at the table and was about to take a sip of the tea he had made with dinner. When suddenly...

BANG! CRASH! THUD!

There came a jumble of noises from the apartment upstairs. Douglas was very annoyed by this, but soon the sounds stopped. He began to take another sip of his tea, when suddenly...

BUMP! ZIP! YAK!

More noises came from the apartment upstairs. Douglas put down his tea in anger. That was enough! All he wanted was a normal dinner, with a normal cup of tea. Was that so wrong?

SLOOSH! SPLOSH! SPLASH!

The noises sounded again. Quickly, Douglas came to a decision. He would go upstairs and politely ask his neighbours to be quiet so he could return to his normal dinner. He was about to take a sip of tea to steady his nerves, when suddenly the tea spoke up.

"Hey, don't drink me!" it screamed.

Douglas paused. "Why not?"

"Would you like to be drunk?" the tea asked. Douglas thought about it. No, he didn't suppose he would like to be drunk. But he still wanted to drink his tea. He would have to be clever.

"But I've got a name," he said craftily. "You don't. It's all right to drink someone if they don't have a name."

The tea spoke up again. "That's some pretty silly logic. But it doesn't matter anyway. I've got a name."

"What is it?" asked Douglas suspiciously.

"It's Winston!"

"Really? That's a bit of a strange name."

"Why?" asked the tea suspiciously.

"Why isn't your name 'Tea'?" asked Douglas.

"Why isn't your name 'Human'?"

Douglas frowned. The tea was being clever. Suddenly the noises sounded again from the upstairs apartment.

WHIZZ! BLORT! SNACKERY!

At that sound, Douglas forgot how much he wanted his tea and remembered how much he wanted to politely ask the people upstairs to be quiet. So he picked up Winston (it seemed rude to leave him behind) and made his way up the long flight of stairs to the upstairs apartment.

Finally, after a minute of climbing, he arrived at the upstairs apartment. He stood at the front door, and more noises exploded from inside.

BUZZ! CRACKLE! POP!

Douglas politely tapped at the door and waited for someone to answer. Heavy footsteps resounded from behind the door, and with a slow creak, it swung open. Much to Douglas's surprise, a large elephant stood at the door and peered down at Douglas and Winston.

"Can I help you?" the elephant asked in a deep voice.

"Whatever you do, don't mention ivory..." Winston whispered.

"Be quiet," Douglas muttered back. That was all he wanted, quiet.

OMNIUM GATHERUM

"What?" asked the elephant, raising a foot to his huge ear.

"I said, could you please be quiet? I can hear you from downstairs," replied Douglas, not quite believing he was talking to an elephant.

The elephant nodded. "If you want us to be quiet, come in and talk to Clarabell. She is the noisiest of us." Suddenly, the elephant sneezed, and a large pair of jeans flew out of his nose. "Sorry, when I got here I never got around to unpacking my trunk." Douglas held Winston close to his chest and gingerly stepped around the elephant into the apartment.

The apartment appeared completely normal, except for the strange noises that were coming from deeper inside. And of course, the elephant, who had taken a seat on the couch in front of the TV, added an aura of oddness to the room. He took out a large handkerchief and blew into it. Out of his nose came a toothbrush and ten rolls of socks.

Douglas politely asked the elephant, "Excuse me, but do you know where I can find Clarabell?"

The elephant shrugged, "Can't remember."

"I thought elephants never forget," Winston piped up.

The elephant shrugged again. "I must have forgotten to remember."

"Or perhaps you remembered to forget?" Winston suggested.

"In that case, I haven't forgotten anything," the elephant replied rather rudely.

Douglas put a hand over Winston's mouth to stop him arguing. "Don't trouble yourself. We'll find Clarabell."

The elephant relaxed and lay down on the couch, taking a remote out from the tip of his trunk. Douglas and Winston walked from the lounge into the kitchen.

The kitchen was alive with activity. Penguin waiters carrying trays of food were waddling left and right, some bumping into each other, all squawking horrendously. In the middle of the kitchen stood a large pot with a polar bear in a chef's hat stirring the contents.

Douglas struggled through the crowd (making sure not to spill

Winston) and went to talk to the chef. The polar bear looked at Douglas and then offered him a ladle of the soup that he was stirring. Douglas tried some; it tasted strongly of fish.

"Excuse me," he asked the polar bear chef politely. "Could you please tell your staff to quiet down?"

"I'm sorry, what?" asked the polar bear chef. He could not hear Douglas over the loud squawk of the penguin waiters.

"I said, could you please tell your staff to quiet down!" shouted Douglas over the din. He was starting to get angry.

Suddenly a penguin waiter waddled up to the chef and pushed a piece of paper into his paw. "Order for table 507," squawked the waiter. The chef ladled some fish soup from his pot into a bowl and handed it to the penguin, who quickly waddled off.

Douglas was starting to become very angry. He hated to be ignored. "Watch what you say to a polar bear," he heard Winston mutter under his breath. Douglas took a deep breath to calm down and asked one more time, "I'm sorry but could you please tell your staff to BE QUIET!"

The polar bear chef sniffed. "No need to shout."

"Well I wouldn't have to shout if everyone would just be quiet," Douglas replied. The polar bear shrugged. "Doesn't matter anyway. I don't deal in sound. I deal in taste. Now if you want your food to taste quieter..."

"No, I don't want anything to *taste* quieter, I want everyone to *sound* quieter," Douglas replied angrily. What was wrong with everyone? He felt like he was going mad.

Suddenly a large BOOM sounded from the soup. Douglas and Winston stared down in amazement and saw a little toy ship floating on top of the soup as if it were an ocean. On the toy boat were little tin soldiers running around the deck and screaming. Much to Douglas's horror, he saw that a squid was attacking their ship! Its tentacles crept up on the deck, grabbing the little tin soldiers and pulling them down into the dark depths of the soup.

"Fire the cannons!" one of the tin soldiers commanded. "Let the

Cracker Kraken taste our firepower!" The tin soldiers fired the cannons with a loud BOOM. But still the tentacles slithered snakelike across the deck. Douglas watched as a slimy tentacle suddenly grabbed the soldier who had been shouting commands. His men wailed with terror and fought back, attempting to free their Captain by firing their tiny muskets. The Captain was slowly being pulled back to the side of the ship. He looked grim and determined to die with dignity.

"You've got to save him!" Winston shouted at Douglas. Douglas hesitated... the cannon fire, the penguins squawking, the tiny screaming... He couldn't think! On impulse, he put Winston down on the floor and plunged his hands into the soup, wrestling the tin Captain from the Cracker Kraken's grip. With the Captain safely in hand, he scooped the rest of the crew off of the sinking ship and placed them all safely down on a nearby table.

The tin Captain bowed low to Douglas and Winston laughing with delight. "Ye saved me and me crew, ye mighty giant. We are in your debt."

Suddenly the polar bear chef began clapping with his great paws and each of the penguins turned to Douglas with surprise. "He saved them," the polar bear chef laughed, astounded. "He saved Captain Pertruzio and his crew from the Cracker Kraken." Suddenly Douglas was surrounded by cheering penguins, each wanting to shake his hand or give him a pat on the back.

"Please, ye honour," said Captain Pertruzio, "if there is any way we could repay our debt?"

"All I want is a little peace and quiet to have my dinner," said Douglas. Winston nodded in agreement with his friend. Captain Pertruzio raised his sword high over his head and pointed at the penguins. "Ye heard him, you barnacle-billed birds; spread the word: Captain Pertruzio says, be quiet so that our hero can dine in peace!" The penguins squawked and fluttered, falling over each other to leave the kitchen and spread the news.

"I'm afraid you'll still have to see Clarabell if you want real peace," said Captain Pertruzio. "It is beyond us to still her noises." The crew bowed their heads in shame, as if by their Captains words, they had failed in fulfilling their debt.

Douglas smiled, "That's okay. You've still been a big help. Do you know where we can find Clarabell?"

The Captain pointed to a door on his left. "Go through that there door, through the room that is for dining, past the toilet and up the stairs. You'll find yer Clarabell." Douglas and Winston thanked him and his tiny tin crew. They scooted around the polar bear chef and through the door to the dining room.

They opened the door to the dining room, and the first thing they heard was a loud BLLENIINTT. Douglas looked surprised (though by now he shouldn't have been) when he saw a cat with a saxophone and a dog with a violin sitting at the dining table talking to each other. The cat counted to three, and they both played their instruments at the same time, making the loud BLLENIINTT sound.

"What are you doing?" asked Winston curiously. The cat and dog looked up and were surprised to see Douglas and Winston standing at the door. "Just jamming, daddio," purred the cat.

"Now don't be modest, Kat," the dog barked and waved a paw at his musical companion. "We're trying to play 'The Greatest Song in the World'."

"True dat, Hond," agreed Kat and tapped his heart twice.

"Can we hear you play it?" asked Winston excitedly.

"But Winston, I came up here to make them quiet down, not get louder," complained Douglas.

Winston looked hurt, "Come on, Douglas. How often do you get to hear 'The Greatest Song in the World'?"

Douglas stopped and thought about it. He supposed you didn't get a chance to hear 'The Greatest Song in the World' very often. "Okay, fine, play away," said Douglas grumpily as he sat down in a chair.

Kat stood up and held his saxophone to his lips. "Okay, Hond, my cool canine compadre, take it from the top." Hond held his violin ready and counted to three.

"Okay... one... two... three..."

BLLENIINTT!

"What was that?" asked Douglas, who was frankly quite bewildered.

Kat put down his saxophone and explained, "That, my brother, was the first note in 'The Greatest Song in the World'!"

"Well, what about the rest of it?" asked Winston disappointedly. He had been expecting more.

"Patience, my tea-leaf tripping associate, we've only got the first note. We'll write the rest of it soon."

"You're trying to write 'The Greatest Song in the World', and you've only got the first note?" asked Douglas dazedly.

"From the start comes the finish," said Hond wisely. "Plus, since we've played the first note, we know the song exists; we just need to play the rest of it."

"Well, do you think you could keep things quiet for a while?" pleaded Douglas. "It's just that I can hear everyone from downstairs, and I would like to eat my dinner in peace."

"No worries, daddio," reassured Kat. "When we play the rest of 'The Greatest Song in the World', you won't hear it in here," he tapped his ear. "You'll hear it in here," he double-tapped his heart.

"Right," said Douglas who wasn't quite sure what he was on about. "Well as long as you keep things down, I'm easy." Kat and Hond began tuning their instruments and seemed to forget that Douglas and Winston were still in the room. Douglas sat in silence for a few minutes and Winston looked at him meaningfully.

"Well, we might as well just toddle off then." Kat and Hond waved their paws in a distracted goodbye, so Douglas picked up Winston and headed for the toilet.

The toilet door was closed, and Douglas could hear noises coming from inside. There was a bang and then some bubbling sounds. Douglas quietly tapped on the door. "Sorry, are you all right?"

"Occupied!" a voice cried out from the toilet. Suddenly there was an even louder BANG, and Douglas stepped out of the way just as the toilet door burst open. A tall man with glasses and blonde frizzy hair fell out of the toilet cubicle and landed on the floor in a heap. He rose to his feet and gave Douglas a funny look. Douglas looked him up and down quizzically. "You're a scientist."

"How do you know that?" asked the man.

"You're wearing a scientist coat," replied Douglas.

"Don't be an idiot. Anyone could buy and wear a scientist coat. It doesn't make me a scientist," the man began to chuckle.

"Are you a scientist?" asked Douglas.

The man paused in mid-snicker. "Well... yes, but you still shouldn't assume such things with little evidence."

Douglas glanced curiously into the toilet room and saw beakers and test tubes stacked onto shelves filled with all sorts of different chemicals. The chemicals in turn seemed to have been poured down into the toilet bowl and the toilet water flashed blue, green, red, indigo, and violet. There seemed to be plenty of evidence to back up Douglas's assumption that the man was a scientist.

"What's your name?" asked Winston politely.

The scientist extended a hand, and Douglas took it. "The name's Barnaby Trump. Barnaby Trump and his famous Educated Guesses."

"The what?" asked Douglas in confusion.

"Ahh, Educated Guesses. You see, some scientists specialize in astronomy or biology. I, however, have a Ph.D. in the regretfully neglected field of Educated Guesses. Look, I have a diploma." He took a piece of paper out of his pocket and unrolled it, showing it proudly to Douglas and Winston. The diploma read:

THIS DIPLOMA HAS BEEN AWARDED TO

OMNIUM GATHERUM

BARNABY TRUMP FOR HIS OUTSTANDING
STUDY IN THE FIELD OF EDUCATED GUESSES.

SIGNED: PROFESSOR PARSELHOUSE ANIMAE

(INSERT INSPIRING LATIN QUOTE HERE.
THANKYOU.)

"You see, any man can make a guess. But it takes an education to make an Educated Guess." Barnaby Trump grinned hugely and rolled up his diploma, placing it back in his pocket.

Douglas rolled his eyes. "That's really great, Barnaby Trump."

"Ahh, Professor Barnaby Trump, if you don't mind. Make sure you enunciate every capital letter."

"Right, well, if you don't mind, I've just got to nip upstairs and..."

"Wait, wait!" cried the Professor.

Douglas sighed, "What?"

"Don't you want me to make an Educated Guess about you?"

Winston jiggled around excitedly. "Oh would you? Would you really?"

"Why of course," smiled Professor Trump modestly. He took out a measuring tape and a strange clicking device. "First the teacup!" Winston smiled excitedly, and Professor Trump measured him lengthways and widthways and sideways. He licked his face, smelled his handle, and ran the clicking device all over his form. Finally, he stopped guessing. "Now if I were to make an Educated Guess," he smiled grandly, "I would say you were a talking teacup. Your contents are precisely two hours old, and you were brewed with a rich Darjeeling teabag."

Winston gasped, "How did you know?"

The Professor looked affronted. "Know? Know? Any man can know and be correct. I made an Educated Guess and was correct. That is something that requires a far greater degree of skill."

Douglas clenched his fists. He was tired of this, and he needed to get upstairs. "Well that was very clever, Professor Trump, but we really do need to be on our way..."

"Ahh, but wait, my dear fellow. Don't you wish for me to make an Educated Guess about you?"

"Not really, I..."

"Ahh, come, come now, it won't take but a moment." The Professor took out the measuring tape and the same clicking device. He measured Douglas lengthways and widthways and sideways. He licked his face, smelled his handle (upon noticing he didn't have a handle, he instead smelled his arm), and ran the clicking device all over his form. Finally, he stopped guessing. The Professor licked his lips and clicked the roof of his mouth. "Ahh, you seem to be a very complex case, my dear fellow. I am about to make an Educated Guess concerning the entirety of yourself, and I must warn you, when I do so, I will be using many complex words and Latin phrases."

"Why?" asked Douglas. Winston was beside himself with curiosity, and Douglas could not help but feel inquisitive.

"Because I am a scientist, and that is what we do," Professor Trump replied simply. He shifted his eyes from side to side; clearly he was about to make an Educated Guess about Douglas that was very interesting. "The problem with you, Douglas, is that you want what you don't have and have what you don't want. Your current circumstance is steeped in thaumaturgically amalgamated activity, and yet..."

Suddenly a penguin waiter rounded a corner and raised a flipper to his beak, shushing the Professor. The Professor broke off and narrowed his eyes in irritation. The penguin squawked, and the Professor nodded his understanding. He made a zipping gesture over his lips. He turned to go back to the toilet, but Douglas reached out a hand to stop him.

"Wait, you can't just stop talking..."

Professor Barnaby Trump sighed and turned to Douglas. He looked him in the eye and gave him a sly wink. He took a pen and a piece of paper from his pocket and quickly scribbled something down. He gave it to Douglas, nodded a goodbye to Winston, and then closed the toilet door, locking it behind him.

"What does it say?" asked Winston curiously. Douglas unfolded the piece of paper and looked at it, reading it aloud. It said:

WHEN IS A DOOR NOT A DOOR?

"I wonder what he means?" whispered Winston wonderingly.

Douglas frowned darkly. "Me too."

Douglas looked up at the stairs worryingly. They seemed very steep and very high. Climbing those steps would be more like climbing a mountain than climbing a flight of stairs. He looked down at Winston, who was clutched tightly by the handle in his fingers. Winston smiled encouragingly, and Douglas smiled back.

"You can do it, Douglas," said Winston confidently.

Douglas took a deep breath and placed his first foot on the staircase. He looked down, and his vision wavered crazily. For some strange reason, the ground seemed very far away. He took another deep breath and firmly gripped the staircase railing. With a burst of courage, he started to climb.

"Winston?"

"Yes, Douglas?"

"What's it like being a talking teacup?"

Winston shrugged as best a teacup could. "Frightening, I suppose."

Douglas looked surprised. "Why?"

"It's not like being a regular teacup. When you can talk, you've also got to listen, think, and choose. It makes the world just a little bit bigger. Sometimes I worry if I'll make the wrong choice."

"Oh," said Douglas worriedly. The two friends climbed in silence for a while.

"Douglas?"

"Yes, Winston."

"What's it like being a talking human?" Douglas shrugged as best a human could.

"Frightening, much like being a talking teacup, I suppose," he said. The two friends climbed in silence for a bit longer.

"Douglas?"

"Yes, Winston?"

"Have you had fun?"

Douglas thought for a minute. He looked back on his encounters in the upstairs apartment. "Let's see, I have so far failed to find Clarabell and get everyone to quiet down so that I can eat my supper in peace. I've been ignored, rudely spoken to, and even terrified. But I've met an elephant who sneezed clothing. Saved a tiny tin Captain from the monstrously miniature Cracker Kraken. Heard the first note in 'The Greatest Song in the World', and met a man who studied the art of Educated Guesses. So yes, I suppose you could say I've had fun."

Winston smiled warmly. "Then you haven't made any wrong choices."

Douglas paused and thought about it. Then suddenly a huge grin stretched over his face, and he hugged Winston close to his chest.

After what seemed like hours but must have been minutes, Douglas and Winston finally reached the top step. In front of them, they saw a long, dark corridor ending in a large oak door. The two friends began creeping cautiously down the corridor. As they approached the door, they noticed three things. The first thing they noticed was that next to the door was a small chair, and on that chair sat an even smaller ragdoll. The second thing they noticed was that carved into the large oak door were strange runes and celestial patterns. The third thing they noticed was that the door was ajar.

"When is a door not a door?" asked Winston quietly.

"When it's a jar," replied Douglas.

OMNIUM GATHERUM

They walked up close to the great door and carefully studied its runes. Douglas noticed that a peculiar-smelling draft was blowing through the door, as if it were an opening to the outside.

"Look!" said Winston wonderingly. Douglas looked down at the small ragdoll and was surprised to find that stitched into the front of its dress was the name:

Clarabell

"Well it looks like we found her," said Douglas thoughtfully as he picked her up from her place on the chair. He remembered the elephant's words, "She is the loudest of us." What a peculiar thing to say about a ragdoll.

Suddenly a loud ROAR sounded from behind the door, and Douglas dropped Winston and Clarabell in fright. Thankfully, the floor was carpeted and soft, so Winston did not break. But the tea that he held spilled messily all over the red carpet. Gingerly, Douglas picked up Winston and held him tenderly in his hands. "I'm sorry," Douglas said worriedly. Winston looked so weak. "I'll pour you another cup!"

Winston laughed feebly, "Don't worry, Douglas, I'm not going to stop talking." Suddenly he let out a loud cough and tea ran in dribbles down his face. "Lo...look at Clarabell," he said quietly. Douglas looked down at the ragdoll that had fallen face-first onto the tea-stained carpet. On her back had been stitched the words:

IF YOU WANT SOME QUIET CLOSE THE DOOR

Douglas hugged Winston close to his chest and placed Clarabell back on her chair. His heart pounding, he put a hand on the door's huge brass doorknob, which was carved in the shape of a lion's snarling face. He was about to close the door when suddenly curiosity seized him, and he cautiously opened it wider, wondering what could possibly be inside.

OMNIUM GATHERUM

This is what he saw. He saw a huge library filled with endless shelves of books. He called into the darkness of the library, and much to his surprise, the books were startled and took flight like frightened birds.

Then his vision blurred.

He saw a great beach with golden sand and a deep emerald green ocean. Titanic dragons played happily in the green alien surf. One seemed to spot Douglas, bellowing mightily in greeting.

Then his vision blurred.

He saw a little girl with stark yellow hair tumbling down an endless rabbit hole.

Then his vision blurred.

He saw a mirror vision of himself holding Winston and slurping tea greedily from his head.

Then his vision blurred.

He saw a band of celestial beings playing elegant instruments for the amusement of the stars.

Then his vision blurred.

He saw the vast ruins of an ancient civilization half buried by a timeless stretch of desert.

Then his vision blurred.

He saw everything that was beautiful, everything that was horrible, everything that was dull, and everything that was inspiring. And he couldn't take seeing any more!

"What is it?" he asked Winston wondrously.

"It's undefinable magic," Winston intoned weakly. "Everything happens somewhere and something happens everywhere." He closed his eyes, as if asleep, and Douglas began to worry that he wouldn't wake up.

He frantically turned his eyes away from the door and picked up Clarabell. "What do I do? What do I do?" Stitched into her back were those same words:

IF YOU WANT SOME QUIET CLOSE THE DOOR

"Will everyone downstairs go away?" Douglas began to horribly suspect. "Will... will Winston go away?"

At that, Winston opened his eyes and said in a voice stronger than Douglas had ever heard him use, "Never!"

Douglas gave his friend one last hug and braced himself against the bizarre celestial carvings of the door. He pushed against it with all his strength and with a loud SQUEAK, the huge heavy oak door swung shut.

Silence was the first thing that Douglas noticed. There was no TOOTING or HOOTING or QUAKING or THUMPING coming from downstairs or behind the door. Douglas laughed, relieved. "Quiet at last, aye Winston?" There was no reply. He held the empty teacup up to his eyes and shook it gently. "Winston? Winston? Are you awake?" The teacup didn't answer. What did was that long sought after silence.

"Winston? Winston? Please answer me. Winston, please," Douglas began to shout. "Please, Winston, you promised you wouldn't leave. You said you wouldn't. You promised!"

Still, the teacup didn't answer.

Furiously he turned on Clarabell and shook her in his hands, shouting at her. "You did this, you took him away! Where is he now? Where is everyone else?"

Douglas threw Clarabell to the floor and took firm grasp of the lion-head doorknob. He began tugging and pulling with all his might. But the door would not budge. "No!" he screamed. "I want the noise back! I want it back!" He looked down to the floor and saw that Clarabell had fallen on her back. Stitched into the front of her dress were the words:

YOU'RE WELCOME

Douglas searched the entire apartment and found it empty. There were no penguins delivering trays of fish soup to mysterious customers, nor any animal musicians. Even the staircase had lost its mountainous height. The apartment was empty, as if what had happened had never been.

Douglas sat in his apartment finishing the last morsels of his cold dinner. The clock ticked constantly and Douglas felt his life settling back into its original boring rhythm. He missed the noise, the adventure, and the strangeness.

But most of all, he missed Winston. The teacup that had been his friend sat empty and clean next to the sink. Douglas had had to scrub him hard to get the tea stains out.

He sighed and collected up his dirty plate and cutlery. As he walked to the sink to wash them, a fork slipped off his plate and fell to the floor. Douglas paused and thought about it. Then he realized something wonderful. He liked the sound!

So he dropped his plate and let it smash on the floor. It made the wonderful crashing sound of cymbals. He banged the table like a drum and tapped his feet like he was wearing tap-dancing shoes.

He walked into his bedroom and jumped up and down on the bed, laughing with joy. He spun the pillows across the room and turned the blanket into a tent.

He went into the bathroom and filled up the bath with water. He took out some dusty toy ships he had received as a present a few years ago and turned his tub into an exciting naval battleground. He saluted merrily, "May the wind blow strong in yer sails, Captain Pertruzio."

He began shouting and singing and dancing. He turned on the radio and boogied down with the music. He whistled along with the tune and double-tapped his heart.

All of a sudden, a loud knock came from his front door. Douglas stopped and was suddenly very embarrassed. He'd been too loud and disturbed the neighbours below him. He crept to the front door and opened it with a sorry smile on his face, ready to apologize.

He gave out a gasp of surprise. In front of him stood a toad in a dressing gown wearing a pair of horn rimmed glasses. The toad put a warty finger to his lips. "Ssssshhhh, could you please quiet down? I'm trying to have my dinner."

Douglas laughed and closed the door. He paused and thought about it. Then he walked back to the kitchen to make himself a cup of tea.

CALLUM DAWSON writes fantasy, fairy tales, and children's stories, and he was the 2012-13 artist in residence for the Faculty of Theology and Religious Studies at KU Leuven. Currently, he is living somewhere between Belgium, Australia, and Fairyland.

TURQUOISE CHILDREN

Turquoise Children is a musician and illustrator who lives in Paris, France with his cat. The pen and ink on paper drawings presented here are from his Storybook series.

OMNIUM GATHERUM

THE AFTERPARTY

Jason Kniep

The idea struck him, probably because a rush of adrenaline was coursing through his body. Or was it oxytocin? Or testosterone? He wasn't quite sure what each of these things did, but something made him feel playful enough to push the nub of the lever and lock all four of the car doors. Daphne stood outside the front passenger door, puzzled by her ineffectual lifting of the door handle. Her handbag had slid to her wrist, and she readjusted it to her shoulder to try opening the door again. Through the glass, he showed her the wide swath of teeth in his spread smile. She looked in at him, frowning. Her voice came through the glass muffled.

"Are you going to unlock it?"

"Oh... I don't know," he said, looking out the windshield in contemplation. Daphne's hand dropped from the door handle, and she turned her head to look down the street. She folded her arms. He looked back at her, still smiling widely, and then flicked the locks open. Daphne, justifiably untrusting, waited before she reached out again for the handle.

"Okay, it's open," he said to her, in a tone suggesting she was being a bad sport.

Also, it was raining.

This was Bill and Daphne's first date, though it was Bill's fifth for the week. He was currently spending $270 each month on dating websites and was determined to get his money's worth. Bill gave his best effort to read the profiles; however, his attempts to keep separate which blond was into water sports and which one was Buddhist became taxing. When such frustrations set in, Bill would take a break and go 'fishing'. Fishing involved sending out a copy-and-pasted note to a wide pool of women, based only on his quick reaction to their photos. Although he was not aware of it, this note was worded in such a way as to make a hopeful person feel that it was personal, much like a horoscope.

Daphne was a fish.

Even his horribly framed, reverse-camera-phone self-portraits could not hide the fact that Bill was an attractive man. His sturdy chin and tailored five o'clock shadow, electric blue eyes, and piles of hair were enough to stop even the most intellectual woman from immediately skipping his profile. And even though intelligence was often claimed as the most important quality, and not looks, Bill was going on a number of dates suspiciously disproportional to the deficiencies in his grammar and spelling. His success on these dates varied, but he had received key tips from the Internet, such as starting the evening with a definitive compliment. This displayed to his date that he possessed the desirable qualities of sensitivity and observation.

Earlier, at their table for two, before he locked Daphne out of his car for fun, he had attempted this very strategy.

"Your hair is beautiful. So red and vibrant. I mean, really stunning." Daphne did not look up from her menu, which sat flat on the table in front of her.

"You read my profile, right?" she said.

"Oh, yeah, man. It was great. They have a salmon here that's Alaskan. I think that means it's especially good." Daphne was watching him scan the menu. She looked around the room, exhaled deeply, and then leaned across the table to speak quietly to Bill.

"You know then, that this is a wig I'm wearing."

"Hmm?"

"My hair is a wig."

Bill was still flipping through his menu when he said, "Where's that damn salmon on here?"

"You didn't read my profile."

"Of course I did. I don't just date anybody."

"And you couldn't remember that this isn't my real hair. That's a big thing to forget."

"I was saying how you can't even tell. How it looks so good and real."

Daphne sat back and considered this. She had a very strong sense that he was lying and hadn't read her profile at all. But his answer was convincing. What if he really was complimenting her wig to try to boost her self-esteem for having to wear one?

So instead of ordering a cab, she decided to order the salmon.

"What kind of wine do you like?" he asked.

"Merlot used to be my favorite. Or a Shiraz. Or a Pinot grigio if white. But I can't drink anymore."

"Listen to you. A connoisseur. We *have* to get some now." He pointed a finger into the air and turned to make eye contact with a waiter.

"Yes, but I just said I can't drink any."

"Of course you can. Or are you an alcoholic?" He said this last part with a laugh as if such a thing could not be possible.

"I can't drink alcohol because of the treatments," she said, but Bill was busy ordering a bottle of Cabernet Sauvignon. When the waiter was gone, Bill folded the drink menu and set it down, smiling large and satisfied.

"Now what's that?" he asked, picking up the conversation.

"You did not read my profile. I have fucking cancer."

"Oh." Bill's face turned serious as he contemplated this news. "So... you're just looking for like some last-minute sex then?"

Later, after his playful fingering of the door locks, as he was driving her home, Daphne leaned her head against the window and watched the rain splash against the black city streets. The only sound between the two of them was the woosh of tires through puddles. Daphne's hair was still soaked and beads of water dripped down her sallow cheeks. The problem was that, yes, she just wanted to have sex, and that was why she had accepted a date with this guy. She thought from his profile that he was no more than a handsome idiot. She had not anticipated insensitivity. Now she just wanted kindness, though she would have settled for silence. If he would have said just the bare minimum, a tongueless, smiling, Ken doll, she would have been ready.

She did not look over at him when she said, "I don't want to be alone tonight."

Inside her home, Bill gave insightless commentary to her décor. About how the orange couch was so orange. About the Mondrian print being so modern. About the minor wattage of her touch lamp. Daphne set down her purse and watched him. He displayed a boyish curiosity, as if this was the first time he had set foot inside another person's home.

"My grandparents had this same ceramic monkey." He picked up the piece and held it close to his face. It was a white, skinny monkey, twisted in a cartoonish position, leaning back on its elbows with its legs crossed, a goofy grin spread across its anthropomorphic face. "I used to love this thing." Bill looked over at Daphne and considered telling her that he used to speak to his grandparents' version of the monkey. He quickly decided it would make him look less cool and kept his mouth shut.

He picked up a photograph, put it back down, and moved on to something else. Daphne smiled. It was like something in him from before had drained off: whatever that chemical is in men that makes them want to fuck everything. Or was he nervous?

Later, he said, "I don't usually blow my wad that fast, but you've got an amazing kit." They were lying on their backs in the semi-darkness, an uninvited streetlight finding its way into the bedroom through the mini-blinds. He was right, it wasn't much.

"I've been going on a lot of dates lately," Daphne said to her ceiling. "My psychiatrist says this is normal. Or for some women it is. Others do the opposite and hole up by themselves. But some of these guys I'm getting with, I've been inviting to this party I'm having."

"Sounds fun."

"You're not invited."

"Oh."

"I'm not sure why I just told you about it. I haven't even told my shrink."

"I promise I won't tell."

"What's the point of even going to one?" she said.

"Parties are fun. I think you'll have a good time."

"I mean my shrink. I just sit there, and she listens and stares at me. And I'm pretty sure she's thinking, 'I'm glad I'm not dying. I'm glad I have a good job and a future and a husband and a small child. I'm at the beginning of my growth potential as a human being. You are at the end, and you didn't do anything. Not even produce a child, which is like the easiest thing in the world for a woman to do.'"

"You really think she's thinking that?" Daphne looked over at Bill, his face silhouetted and furrowed. It may have been the first time all evening that he had listened to what she had said. There was something so childish about this poor guy. Self-centered and insensitive, yes, but also something lonely and neglected. Someone whose parents had repeatedly forgotten to pick him up after school.

After a deep pause, Daphne leaned over to the nightstand and pulled from it a small business card that she handed to Bill.

"Thanks for coming over. I had a good time," she said. Sometimes she had to be blunt, and it didn't take long for her to realize that Bill was going to be one of those times. "I want you to leave now, please."

His belt was still undone and his laces untied when he stepped out into the cold air and heard Daphne's deadbolt slide in behind him. It was late, and the sudden temperature drop awakened him from his post-ejaculatory drowsiness. He was in his car, warming it up, when he examined the business card. It said simply, "The Afterparty by Daphne" and under that, "November 15" and a Web address that ended in "/FAQ."

On November 15, Bill returned to Daphne's house after much

OMNIUM GATHERUM

deliberating. Most of the leaves had fallen from the trees, and those that still clung were only dead dangling scabs on gray branches. Following a frigid October, the weather had turned unusually warm. Winter seemed so far away, almost impossible.

There were already several people inside. At the far end of the living room, there was a bar set up in front of a bartender serving drinks. An Elvis Presley record was playing on the turntable. Bill made straight for the bar, a limited selection of nothing but wine. In the dining room, he spied a table of cheese platters, stacked fruits, and thinly-sliced deli meats. A man in the same outfit as the bartender, jacketless in a black bow tie and cummerbund, tapped Bill on the shoulder.

"Excuse me, sir. I just saw you come in."

"Yes. Oh, yes."

"Here's your number." The man handed Bill a little slip of 80lb card stock with the number '14' on it, embossed in gold. Bill tried to remain suave but emptied half his wine glass in the first sip.

She was much thinner than he remembered, but she didn't seem sick, lying there. Her body didn't look skeletal or overly ravaged by disease. And there was something else different about her that he couldn't put his finger on. The light in the room came from a single table lamp, a dim wattage. Everything else about the room was as he remembered it from a few weeks earlier except for a lingering heavy scent. Not the antiseptic sting of hospital cleaners but a pleasant floral aroma. Was it lilacs or magnolias, this scent? He stood over Daphne, looking down and trying to think whether or not he would recognize her if he saw her on the street. The room was cold, and she looked cold. Her eyes were closed, her red wig fanned out behind her head like old paintings of goddesses being born on the waves of a sea.

He had done the math while waiting in the living room with his second glass of wine. He was number 14, and at ten minutes a pop, that meant by the time he would see her, she would have been dead almost two and a half hours.

He slipped off his shoes, unbuckled his belt and began undoing the buttons of his shirt, starting from the top, all the time watching Daphne's quickly cooling, naked body lying on the bed. There were sanitizers and towels on the bedside table. I am number 14, he thought.

FAQ #1: But isn't that prostitution?
Prostitution involves the exchange of money for sexual acts. There is no money involved.

When he was naked, he lay down beside her, placing the palm of his left hand across the bone of her hip. The crenelations in his knuckles and the bulging of blood vessels on the back of his hand appeared magnified against Daphne's smooth skin. Her dead young waist and his steadily aging hand. She had taken good care of herself. Probably used moisturizer regularly. And this was what it came to. Bill's shoulders had contracted tightly up against his neck, and he attempted to relax them. He closed his eyes and inhaled the perfume she was wearing. She must have dabbed that on herself. Before.

FAQ #2: Isn't that illegal?
The documents you and I sign beforehand will show unequivocally that we each enter into this agreement with full consent.

The room was quiet, sealed and still, a carpeted, echoless chamber. No noise could be heard coming from the living room. He wasn't sure he wanted to do this, but he was sure he had to do it. If life presents you with an opportunity for new experience, you must grab it. Right?

His hand moved up her hip bone to her abdomen and ribs and stopped. His warm breath was reflecting off her neck and back into his face. Everything else was cold. His penis remained a shriveled nub.

OMNIUM GATHERUM

FAQ #3: How does it work?

The lethal injection terminating my life will be administered at 3pm by my doctor. My lawyer will be present to oversee the "festivities" and make sure the scheduled encounters of ten minutes apiece are strictly adhered to. Johnson & Sons will handle the catering: hors d'oeurves and wine.

Bill's warm tears dotted the dark sheets. His chest was tight, but he made no sobs, no sound at all. He had not moved from his curled position at her side, his hand draped across her ribs. He heard the sound of a light tinkling alarm that indicated the seven-minute mark, the strict warning to get dressed. How can it be over already, he thought.

FAQ #4: But why?

I have been an organ donor all my life, and I was disappointed to learn that by the time of my death, none of my organs would eligible for donation. I never thought much about what it meant to be a donor until recently. After death, what happens to them is of no concern to me. My body is relinquished to whatever use can be made of it, sliced up and divvied out to the needy.

*I created my dating profile with that in mind. That I **do** have something to give. I'm sure I am the only woman who listed "necrophilia" under her list of interests, and this touch seemed to be enough to draw each of you out for a date. So far, it seems to be working. We reach an understanding. And it feels good to know I can give you something that remains out of reach in your day-to-day living.*

So I'm throwing this brief and limited party for you. For you to use all of my organs one last time in a state that only you have need for. It is with this spirit of charity that I say to each of you: fuck me.

Dressed and moving down the hallway, Bill attempted to hide the fact that he was wiping tears from his cheeks with the back of his shirt sleeve. A short man, number 15, approached. He and Bill scooted past each other with efficient anonymity, eyes averted, but an odd and tiny tattoo on the man's neck of a mouse playing an oboe caught Bill's attention.

As Bill stepped out into the bright light of the living room, he heard the door to Daphne's bedroom close behind him. His chest was still tight, his head now pounding. Which chemical was going through his brain to cause this feeling? Epinephrine? Vasopressin? It was like something had got inside of him. Like he had been injected. He began scratching his head, his arms, his legs. He turned his mottled face towards a bookshelf, away from the hovering caterers who were beginning their cleanup duties and sneaking cheese. Bill sniffled and rested his forehead on a shelf. He knew he had to pull it together and get out of the house quickly, in one swift movement. He opened his eyes to gather his strength and saw, inches in front of him, the smiling grin of Daphne's white ceramic monkey. Bill's breathing slowed. He looked into the beady, painted dots that were shorthand for monkey eyes.

"I thought I could do it," he whispered to the monkey.

"I know you did, buddy," the monkey whispered back. "Don't worry about it. I still think you're the coolest guy in the world."

———————

JASON KNIEP lives in Lawrence, Kansas, USA with his dog, Bowie.

SHE AND I

Jessica Poelmans

She and I. Us. That's how it would be. That's how it should be. But unfortunately, that's not the way the world in which we live works. This world evolves, and although we often don't realize it, we are drawn into this vortex that we so arbitrarily have called 'evolution.'

Evolution. The mere thought of it makes me feel ill at ease. And yet I cannot escape it. This dirty word, which for me has an almost obscene meaning, turns up unannounced in my still strongly-guarded mind. It creeps into my thoughts, silent as the night, and makes me fix my attention on everything that has changed.

Nothing is the same, and nothing will every be the same again. It confirms that my precious memories are relegated to oblivion. That I, as a human being, am not strong enough to hold on to that which once had been most dear to me, but that I, and everyone else for that matter, am powerless to the dictatorial regime which is this evolution.

We were brought up this way. From the very outset, we were almost conditioned to stay together. Be at one with each other. That is how we were taught to face this cruel world. Thus, growing up, I believed this eternal union to be a logical line of argument.

She didn't. She was well-adapted to the surroundings, which to me felt nearly jungle-like, a petrified jungle deprived of all vivaciousness. Not her. Change and evolution did not knock her off balance at all. She faced them courageously, with her head held high. But I believe that she, armed with her shield of endless bliss and her sword of positiveness, she can conquer anything.

I, however, don't adjust easily. Fear often owns me, possesses my entire being, hanging over me like a dark shadow, like a vile body-odor one cannot get rid of, stunting my personal growth. Because of this – I can't understand why – from childhood on, they taught me that she was to be forever by my side, and then, when all grown-up, they tell me to let her go. We are both supposed to find someone else and go our separate ways with our new partners. Walk into the sunset with them. Sad to say that they didn't make me acquainted with this little fact.

I am not the kind of person who handles these things well, who can handle these things at all, really. Ever since childhood, they taught me that I would be able to hold my own against this cruel world just because she was there, right next to me. And then, all of a sudden, I have to let her go. I have to cope on my own. Alone. And she, she is supposed to spread her wings, walk into the sunset with someone else, leaving me behind. They didn't tell me about that at all. Nobody did.

But then it happens. Suddenly. He joins my universe, softening everything as he enters. The scalding lump of fury in my stomach gives out, gives up, gradually. And the terror of him replacing her, like I always believed he would replace me too, fades away. She and I will not become he and I. No. She and I remain what we have always been: us. Inseparable, irreplaceable.

I finally get it now. Freedom, nimbleness, light fills the world I have considered to be so vile. Tears fill my eyes, but they are not the same tears as before. These tears have extinguished the fire inside me, the fire that has marked my existence so strongly since the very beginning. These tears bring along calm and understanding, a clear hand and a pure heart.

And even though evolution and I will never become close friends, I learned that everything is what it becomes. And that it is not all wrong. Change exists, but she and I, we remain. I am not ready to let her go, not now, not ever. And I will never have to.

OMNIUM GATHERUM

JESSICA POELMANS studies philology at KU Leuven in Belgium. She revels in language and culture and has recently spent several months living in Spain.

WOODEN EYES

Photograph by Sara Rich

HUMAN GLITCH

Alexandria Somirs

Glitches come naturally to all earthlings,
above and below and in the in-betweens.
Some of us too small and some too be big,
some too hard and others too soft.
And others too wet while others too dry.
There are those of us who won't walk, but reach up for the sky,
and others who run, searching for their appetite.
As one species multiplies and the others divide,
programmers beyond sought equal sides.
But the biggest atrocity of humankind is a little thing called curiosity.
With one itchy bite, one idea chases another and that another,
all spilling out unsatisfied.
We twist and bend and stretch and end the very limitations
of our earthly foundations.
Without restraint we sometimes forget that we are
but mere earthlings ourselves and not robotic demigods.
Our natural governing laws growing ever flawed,
tainted with a false sense of progress, as normality becomes excess.
Starting at our feet we walk on hard concrete.
Moving up to our knees we bend with less ease.
Our somewhat small belly grows and expands to unsatisfied ends into
something quite helly.
Our big heart, soft and tender changes to something quite
hard and slender.
Our arms become stiff, our ancient understanding hieroglyphed,
unable to reach out to our human-sided doubts.

Our head too neo growing with our boundless ego,
but just shy of defection keeping away common connection.
Not enough room for too much compassion and not enough room
for too much likeness.
We sometimes forget we are but mere earthlings
and not robotic demigods,
but there are some natural glitches that can be fixed.

ALEXANDRIA SOMIRS tries to capture a unique reality with her writing. Currently based in Leuven, Belgium, her international background helps her to look at life through the eyes of people from different corners of the world.

INCREDULOUSLY

Katelynne Davis

A lot of people can say they've had a crisis of identity in college. It's almost as much a cliché as the ramen. But I'm confident that my story about this collegiate rite of passage is unique. To begin with, I was not discovering a new part of myself, but something I wasn't.

When I was eight and a half, my parents got the happy news that my social ineptitude and hyperbolic bookishness came with a disorder whose name leads to hilarious if disturbing Google searches. Relieved, we settled into the new title, buddying up with Einstein and a host of later famous 'Aspies' (as we in the community refer to ourselves): Temple Grandin, Daniel Tammet, Sheldon Cooper.

Or so we thought.

The Americans With Disabilities Act passed the same year I was born and includes the recently recognized diagnosis of Asperger's Syndrome. (It has since become a 'fad-syndrome', but I was there before it went mainstream.) The ADA built upon precedent legislation, such as The Rehabilitation Act of 1973, which includes my lifelong companion, Section 504. This section declared illegal any discrimination because of disability (and yes, it took us until 1973 to officially write this). Part of Section 504's implications establishes the requirement to provide accommodations for disabled persons, securing their right to participate on an equal basis with the non-disabled.

504 Plan-type accommodations include ramps for wheelchair-access, for example, but there are a lot of us covered under the ADA: physical, mental, learning, and social disabilities (mine is the last). I had

accommodations all throughout school, ensuring I could learn with my classmates despite difficulties with the irregular synaptic makeup of my brain. For example, at the beginning of high school, I still had such problems with fine-motor development that my fingers were too feeble to peel off the plastic covers on pudding packets. This resulted in wretched handwriting (which was nothing to the agony of unattainable pudding), so I was allowed a computer to type all my final exams. Each September, my parents met with my teachers and explained the procedures involved with their little Aspie darling. And every few years, I would take a new psychological evaluation which would test me for presumably relevant but seemingly erratic capabilities. (I was once tested to see how long a sequence of numbers I could accurately repeat backwards. I scored "Extremely High Capacity." If this Master's Degree doesn't work out, I might just take that one on the road.)

But college years are the threshold of independence, and my parents would no longer do the advocating for me. I had to go to the Disabilities Department myself. There was one benefit of this responsibility: for the first time, I could look at my own handful of psychological evaluations from the past decade. Imagine hearing people talk about you without knowing you're listening, and that's close to the feeling of reading your own Psych Eval. I started from that first diagnosis, age eight and a half, reminiscing about the odd life of little Katie and reading myself from the psychologist's eye.

At the end of his report, Dr. Green had concluded, "Katelynne displays several symptoms of a social development disorder, such as Asperger's Syndrome, but further observation should be conducted before a formal diagnosis is made." The next form in my file was a session I had with a different child psychologist some years later, and so went the next, right up to my "Extremely High Capacity" in reversing numbers. But I was missing the formal diagnosis. I called my mom to remind her that she forgot the most important part of my file.

"Oh, we never got that. Once we heard from that first doctor, I looked up 'Asperger's Syndrome', and I knew it was right."

My mother is a teacher with a background in childhood education, but she is by no means a psychologist. It was the era of increasing popularity and curiosity about the autistic spectrum, accompanied by epiphanous self-diagnoses and declarations of Asperger's. And I had no official documentation to say I was the real thing. Even worse – I was mom-diagnosed.

When I was too young to really understand it, 'Asperger's Syndrome' were two words that relieved my parents. It meant they were not failures, that my persistent bizarrity was not a direct result of some atrocious parenting. It meant there were other mothers who had hand-flapping, Lion-King-fixated children with academic vocabularies. It meant there was research and developmental breakthroughs and federally mandated help. For myself, I grew into Asperger's as part of my identity. It was a stamp of permanent specialness – for better or worse, I never had to worry if I was 'just like everybody else'. I was provably neurologically atypical! No hum-drum commonality for me, I was (almost literally) hard-wired to be different.

But then, without that formal diagnosis, the surety was gone. Suddenly, an unthinkable possibility: that I no longer sat in a category with Albert Einstein and Henry David Thoreau, that I could not count on my very synapses to account for uniqueness. That I had no reason for social awkwardness but my own shortcomings. That I was now simply unaccountable. Hans Asperger had been my relief for a long time, and now his assurance was gone.

In itself, it was a surreal crisis of identity – you're NOT strange! Or rather you are, but you no longer have any explanation why. Perhaps there's something just outright wrong with you? I began to wonder how much of my life had passed through this placebo effect. I saw prefigurations throughout my past – when I met other people with Asperger's, hadn't we always been annoyed with each other? And how come I so often functioned better than they did? Now I knew – because I was normal. Mediocre, median, conventional, conforming, neurotypical, normal.

Needless to say, this depressed me.

In life, unlike fiction, I cannot not give a nicely-wrapped ending even if I wanted. To date, I still have not seen a new psychoanalyst for an official diagnosis. I'm scared to. This Syndrome with a name like a horrible derriere-disfigurement is too much a part of me. I eventually came to the firm conviction that Hans Asperger's titular discovery does describe me, based on the obsessive-repetitive habits I had as a kid, some of which persist and some of which I grew out of, many too embarrassing to recount. And I don't believe a series of respected schools would agree to provide accommodations if my behavior did not give off a strong sense of autism. But I still can't bear to face the possibility that we were wrong. I don't know if I'll ever have that courage.

I do know that I will likely encounter disbelief among my readers, and I have come across skeptics in my off-paper life as well. But to those who say, "I never knew/don't think you have Asperger's," I invariably reply:

"Whenever people tell me that I just look at them incredulously."

"Why?"

"Because I just used the world 'incredulously' in a casual sentence and you didn't think I had Asperger's?"

KATELYNNE DAVIS is flexing old, stiff, and underused writing muscles after a long hiatus. She has had non-fiction and photographs published in *The Catharsis* and several articles on Mannix Marketing Inc. websites before her long break, and she hopes that her return to the ring will make for a dramatic and triumphant comeback worthy of a Stallone film.

BETWEEN THE TREES

Photograph by Sara Rich

JOHN DONESTRE

Sara Rich

Her walk was brisk as the day was too. The days were so short this time of year, with the shortest of them all only a week away.

Her thoughts were preoccupied elsewhere. As Christmas drew near, and Thanksgiving was over, she felt even more the foreigner, separated by an ocean and three languages from the hot hedge-burning fireplace that kept her family's ranch house warm during wind-strewn and ice-ridden winters on the Great Plains.

As she walked, the cobblestones closing and counting the distance between her flat and the brick walls of the library, urine-soaked by decades of seven-a.m. drunks, she heard loneliness stumbling along after her, disguised as yellowed leaves whirling toward the backs of her feet.

New Years Day would mark nine days until five years of being in this country: this country that seemed incessantly devoid of warmth even in the sweaty heights of summer. Winters made it remote and desolate even though Christmas markets burgeoned with fondue and fresh waffles and Glühwein. This place was packed with people, not a one of them to be bothered with the existence of the next.

The park was still open, and she decided to cut through it since dusk was ascending rapidly across the eastern sky, chasing out that last dirty bit of sunlight that only served to highlight the dinginess of the village and its unresponsive, defeatist post-war architecture. The park was also the only place on her flatward path where she could choose to walk in grass instead of stone or concrete. Although cold and wet, the grass and the earth it grew out of gave her feet a sense of being warmed and welcomed, grounded knowing that at least grass and mud are the same everywhere, practically.

A man's shape was silhouetted against the light falling from a street lamp, and the silhouette grew bigger as they walked toward each other, toward opposite entrance and exit points of the park. As they came closer together, his silhouette gained shape and color. He wore beige corduroys and a hip-length navy-blue jacket, but she still noticed that beneath those winter layers was well-formed man. His stride was confident without arrogance, strong without brutality. He had a five o'clock shadow that made a whisker-frame around a healthy-lipped mouth and made his square jaw and aquiline nose more prominent. His tawny hair was longish and thick, like the mane of some Serengeti lion or a once-thought-extinct ancestor. His eyes were primeval orange-brown and glowed like a hedge-burning fireplace. She found herself smiling.

"Good evening," he offered first, and she immediately detected a familiar twang in his words. "I don't reckon you've got the time, do you?" He smiled, lips closed and a little dry.

"Oh, sure." She pulled back the left sleeve of her jacket and pushed up the rim of her glove. "It's 4:32."

"Gonna be dark soon, I guess."

She smiled again, teeth exposed. "Yeah, any minute now." He glanced skyward, curiously, and she asked, "Sorry to be nosy, but where are you from?"

"Kansas, born and raised. You?"

"Me too," she said, the latter word stretched out into two excited syllables. "I guess international Kansans are a rare breed. Are you studying here?"

"Yep, sure am. Linguistics. How 'bout you?"

"History. Early-modern European," she clarified. "What part of Kansas are you from?"

"By the sound of it, same as you. Southwestern part, just a little north of the Panhandle."

"This is just uncanny!" She nearly trampled over him like one of those yellowed leaves, eager for familiarity and non-loneliness and a trip, no matter how fleeting, back to the prairie from the other side of this marble-small world. "Will you get to go home for Christmas?"

"Not this year. Too much work to do. So you live around here?" His tone was friendly, inquisitive, genuine.

"Yeah, just a little ways beyond the park."

"Oh, pardon me. Name's Donestre. John Donestre." He extended a hand, ungloved and warm, and she took it with hers and thought she could feel smooth, clean fingernails and strong work calluses beneath her black faux-leather.

"I'm Kristin. It's really nice to meet you. Donestre sounds French, maybe. Do you have family here?"

"Nope. The name's Anglo-Saxon, and I'm here alone." As he said it, with a stolid resignation, she had a sudden need to accompany him everywhere, to alleviate his aloneness as he would hers. She felt she knew that this chance encounter was happening for a reason, that fate was forming a magnet that would draw them together and would refuse them to ever separate again, like they were meant to be together from birth or even conception, and somehow, across thousands of miles and a few decades, they had found each other, and the miles and years no longer mattered at all.

"I don't suppose you'd want to come over for a cup of coffee? My place is just around the corner, on the other side of the park. I bet we'd have a few things to talk about." His invitation fell on greedy, blushing ears.

"Sure, I'd love to," she said, trying in vain to hide her enthusiasm.

He smiled, lips parted this time, also trying in vain to hide his enthusiasm. She shyly looked away before noticing how the street lamp reflected off white, polished teeth that ended in little points like those of carnivores. The incisors tilted back slightly and elevated the canines, lending a feline character to his modestly obscured smile.

At his apartment, he opened the door for her, and she entered. She liked this old-fashioned, chivalrous gesture. The furnishings were sparse and the walls decorated only in age-old paper with a fleur-de-lis print. No photos or paintings, but there was a bookshelf on the opposite wall. She wandered closer just long enough to make out that they were multilingual volumes, some in scripts unrecognizable, the kinds of books belonging to a linguist or a collector.

"It's so nice and warm in here," she observed while removing her gloves and shoving them into her coat pockets.

"Yeah, it's good to be in out of the cold." He blew on his hands and rubbed them together, exaggeratedly since they hadn't really been cold before. "Here, I'll take that," he said and hung Kristin's coat on a hook behind the closed and locked door and placed his own on top of it. "Make yourself at home. I usually make it pretty strong; is that all right?"

"You read my mind. And just black, please, no milk or sugar." She sat down on the loveseat, upholstered in floral tapestry with little creatures, foxes and peacocks, intermittently woven between the plants. "This couch is fabulous. Is it old?"

He filled a teapot with water and set it on the gas stove and answered, "Yeah, it's pretty old. Well, you're the historian; I guess you could tell me."

Kristin laughed humbly. "I don't know that much about antique furniture, but judging by the orange and brown color scheme, it might be from the 60s."

"It's a lot older'n that. Have a look at the woodwork." He dropped three spoonfuls of coffee grounds into the French press.

She examined the intricate scrollwork on the back, arms, and legs. Although it was smooth and delicate, the wood also appeared strong and unchanged – no sticky layers of varnish or splintered rosettes. "Is it mahogany?"

"Straight out of the Belgian Congo. Before it was the Belgian Congo."

"When the whole area was privately controlled by King Leopold II," she mused. With her index finger, she traced the outline of a woven yellow leopard peering down from the branches of a tree. "So it's turn-of-the-century. And in such good condition." Since knowing its antiquity, her admiration for the settee was compounded, as if the aged furniture were binding the centuries and continents together. The world was minute and conquerable again. And somehow, by his awareness of this history, she felt even more validated in her attraction to this very familiar stranger. Someone else who appreciated relics; in fact, his whole apartment, and he himself, seemed somewhat anachronistic, folkloric in a modern age. And yet he, the fellow Midwesterner displaced, did not seem out of place in this environment, like she still did but did not want to be.

He joined her on the loveseat and handed her the coffee in an old white porcelain cup, fissured minutely with time and heat-release like dry skin on the back of a winter hand. "You know, I still make sun tea in the summers," he said meekly, like he was at a confessional.

She smiled collaboratively. "Me too. When the opportunity arises between cloud cover." Then the words came stumbling out before she could stop them, those yellow-leafed words seeking an immediate remedy to loneliness.

"I hope this doesn't sound too weird, but I feel like I know you. Or knew you, before. I went to school in Garden City. Is it possible we knew each other there? It's just that I feel so – It's just that you're so – " She shook her head slowly and took a deep breath, looking for the right, least-incriminating words.

"Comfortable? Familiar? That doesn't sound weird to me at all." The warmth in his eyes was reassuring, and the corners of his mouth lifted.

She looked down shyly, sipped the last of her coffee, and set the empty cup on the table, which was an antique leather-bound travel trunk, another relic of transience transformed into a stationary and satisfied servitude.

"I know we just met, but I hope you'll stay for dinner." He cleared his throat and added quietly, "And I don't want you to leave." He set his still-full cup on the trunk next to hers. With his hands free, he reached over and gently touched her light brown hair, straight and short-cropped. "You're so familiar to me," he said softly, almost a whisper. His hands enveloped the sides of her face, and she'd never felt so admired or adored. She'd never felt so known.

She looked into his hedge-burning eyes and made no attempt to speak. She could not speak, although they had promised each other conversation. Her tacit response was confirmation enough that she would be staying for dinner, for the night, for ever. He held the back of her head and kissed her, and she succumbed to the weight of his lips, the tickling of his whiskers, and the sharpness of his teeth. They made love, and she knew that she would never be alone again, that she would be with him always, their bodies conjoined into a single timeless, spaceless entity.

Afterward, the coffee's effect came, and she became comatose. He carried her to the bathtub, pressed against his bare chest and cradled in his arms, and placed her in the basin, elevated by four white clawed feet cast in iron.

He started with her belly, ravenous. His face stained sanguine, his beard dripping with her blood and viscera, he gnawed through her midsection with irreducible hunger. He took no time to lick his lips or wipe them with the back of his hand: her heart was still beating, the entrails still warm and the blood still rushing.

She had eaten an apple for lunch, and he could taste it, sweet and ripe.

As he lapped up the blood pooling in the half-eaten cavity, her heart stopped beating.

Even with her yet-warm bowels completely masticated, he was still famished. Limb by limb, he licked the bones clean before crunching them too between his polished leonine incisors.

When he had finished, he leaned back from the blood-painted bathtub, panting, his own bowels full to bursting. Her head lay in the basin, face drained pale and porcelain, and eyes closed with the peaceful look of someone whose last thoughts had been of knowing what it means to be beloved. With great affection and tenderness, he reached his hands out to her and stroked her hair, so familiar. Carefully, he picked up her head, face cradled in crimson hands, and held it to his heart as though he could make love to her again. He kissed the coldening lips, gently but fully. And as he did so, he began to weep. He pressed her hair and tender, dead face against the side of his neck and embraced it tightly as he cried, wetting the soft brown hair with twin salt-water rivers and her own blood. His hunger for human companionship was satiated for now. But while he would feel the emptiness and longing again within a few short days, she would never be alone. And for that, he envied her.

OMNIUM GATHERUM

SARA RICH writes speculative fiction between editing gigs and archaeology digs. Her recent novel, *Ligatures*, is now available through Chupa Cabra House.

INEVITABLE DIALECTICS OF THE LITTLE FOXES THAT SPOIL THE VINE

Michael Ayomipo Akinbolusere

Feelings – not like a serene pavilion,
Which seems to incur the realm of oblivion;
Soaked in a timeless state of unconscious consciousness,
In which my body, spirit and mind partitions;
Constantly seeking for a glimpse of happiness,
My soul thou resiliently petitions.

From cradle to grave – an inevitable brief feeling,
Indicating from time to time an unwarranted state;
Sometimes consistently rearing its ugly head to the ceiling,
From the past transcending up to date.

From cradle to grave – an inevitable plight,
Seldom instigating speechless words;
Far from a state of wanted delight,
But restless mood of moulds.

On one hand less tiring – physically, socially, and mentally…
On the other more strenuously psychological and emotional;
In its constant disturbing manifestations,
Features of unnecessary human premonitions.

In every recurring chant of every unfortunate… crass?
Laments: hopefully this too shall pass.

Let me be, in peace, oh! Let me be!
Celebrates after it finishes its cause unduly;
Beseeches by beckoning thee… anticipated feeling,
Like Paul's blissful believing.

So unsure, and yet seemingly so real,
This terrestrial–directed mirage surreal;
For the wicked do sometimes flee,
When no man pursues its fleece.

Lord knows, I have a recurring, realm of dreams,
Which by and by seems to be filled with esteemed steams;
Oh this foggy, imagery of abject bliss on screen,
Like the ones I sight on magazines.

Will this linger and succeed?
Me; and allow me all my life essence bleed?
Oh how I do love to hide or heed,
To every life's book I read;
Yet can't seem to quench these needs,
In speed and in solemn greed in all my deeds;
Do sway my character's worth,
Whence a voice cries out henceforth:

Chitter chatter, chitter chatter,
Nobody's secret is safe with you;
You listen discretely to every stutter,
To your ears all tales seem to glue;
Every tale like added sweetener or sugar,
Embellished with a juicy detail or two;
A cluster of gist, never in speech so frugal,

OMNIUM GATHERUM

Do take in listening some clues & cue;
Your resonating nineteen eighty-seven contagious gloom,
Before it seals our fate to a foreseen cantankerous doom.

Oh how I do yearn to hide or heed,
The book of life I piously read;
Un-seemingly quenching these ignited carnal needs,
In degree and creed of all my deeds.

Behold, solace which doesn't grow on trees,
Ushering rest-spite like gates opened without... keys;
Do we eternally pursue profane greens?
Wallowing and revelling in blissful scenes.

Oh bringer of peace let's make a bond like a team,
A covenant that is flexibly steady;
Like mother nature's beam.
Ha…ah it's high time already,
That we were paired like the eyes we use to see;
And be vast in strength like the deep blue sea.

What is life if not a soothing breeze,
That perhaps seems to instil temporary laze;
And what is life if not limited immortality,
That seems to be devoid of eternity.

I venture to step outside my bubble,
Because man must surely die... our careless trouble;
Constantly placing mind over matter,
And spirit before flesh; a flowing living water.

OMNIUM GATHERUM

In the very depths of my being's intentions,
Never given into fear and speculations,
Although, I wrestle with principality,
I tread on Babylon with musicality.

My world, the word recreates,
Being a student of life's philosophy;
Not falling prey to frivolities,
Or to the deceiver who deceives the deceit.

He says: Occupy till I come,
I pray thy kingdom comes.
When am weary or faint at heart,
To the weak He gives strength.

My comforter, my helper,
There is none like you.
My teacher, my reminder,
Your vessel readily awaits you.

My redeemer, my keeper,
I daily do adore you.
My king and master,
Your servant finds freedom in you.

My father, my Creator,
Your child's obedience is inclined to thee.
Ancient of Days, 'I Am That I Am',
The windows to my soul are set upon thee.

Beatitudes of blissful eternal life,

OMNIUM GATHERUM

No end to which I cleave.
As above, so below; may it be so…
Eledumare (God) my soul prays… it is so!

MICHAEL AYOMIPO AKINBOLUSERE is from Ondo, Nigeria, grew up in Lagos, and currently lives in Belgium, where he studies philosophy and business marketing. Alongside freelance writing and photography, he enjoys drama, dance, and fabric design.

TURQUOISE CHILDREN II

IT LOOKS LIKE I'M GERMAN NOW

Daniel Tkatch

I would much prefer to have a bear on my new German passport than this golden eagle. But not the bear from Berlin's flag – the one with claws, teeth, and a sticking-out tongue – I'd rather have the one in green patina, like the little bronze bear on the central reservation of the A115 autobahn at the former East-West border checkpoint, Drei Linden. Greeting him, any time I leave Berlin or arrive back, holds a sentimental pleasure for me. But what is it that bothers me about the German federal eagle?

When I look at it now, it makes me think of my Russian grandmother, even though it's not even World War II. In our family, no one had suffered from the Germans directly. But she, born in 1931 in a village in Ingushetia, was evacuated as a child from the approaching Caucasus Front. Her father, my great-grandfather, whose name I was given, always carried a handkerchief wrapped around his right hand. When I asked my grandmother about it, she said that they were starving without the breadwinner at home, so he shot through his right palm with a rifle in order to be released back, thus also escaping an almost certain death at the front. And she told me that we should never speak of it again.

It was also she who tried to shape my openness to other cultures and nationalities from an early age. She used to cite her own grandfather: "Any evil person is an enemy to me, but a good one, whoever he may be – a Chechen or even a German – is but a brother." This is why I'd be glad to talk to my grandmother about my recently becoming German, but alas, she passed away nine years before the spring during which I bought a return flight ticket to Germany only to let the flight back expire. For now, I have to face the eagle issue on my own. But I just can't help finding that poor bird too heraldic, too patriotic.

Instead of turning German, I think I would much rather become a plain-vanilla citizen of Europe. Maybe that could liberate me from the bells and whistles of a nation state. It would be much easier for me to identify with the abstraction of the so-called European idea. On a daily basis, however, my identification problem just needs a superficial solution. After all, most people for whom my nationality is of any concern are only interested in its utterly superficial component, which can be sufficiently attested by an ID.

Writing these lines, I come to realize that I have become German, at least to the extent that my Germanness does now seem to pose a problem of some sort. For example, despite my rational understanding of the seriousness of the historical issue with World War II, I always found it a bit alienating that the Germans never laughed or even smiled when I used to tell them about my first experiences with the German language. My first German words were *Achtung, Hände hoch,* and *Hitler kaputt.* I picked them up from other kids when we played 'fascists and partisans' in the street. But as this fact seemed to be of no amusement to most Germans, including the younger ones, I stopped mentioning it altogether. Back when the film *Inglourious Basterds* was released in Germany, I immediately bought a ticket for the screening in one of the biggest cinemas in Berlin: Kino International on Karl-Marx-Allee. I did it intentionally. I wanted to see the film in a big cinema, among a crowd of Germans. And what a joy, what an incredible relief it was to me each time they laughed at this film's trashy depiction of World War II. But do I, having now become German, today suffer from the very complex that has irritated me all these years? Why can't I just accept it? Would becoming, say, Latvian cause the same amount of obsessive introspection?

* * *

My first attempts to be a patriot are a bit of an embarrassment for me today. I was born in the Kazakh Soviet Socialist Republic, and one of my earliest memories from school is the lucid joy as we read about Grandpa Lenin in the first grade ABC book. I was full of gratitude to this wonderful man, happy and proud to have been born in the Soviet Union, not having to become a son of slaves in the gloomy and corrupt West. Soon after that came the early 1990s. And, as Lenin was experiencing a second death and it was going pretty much downhill with my Soviet homeland in general, my parents decided to immigrate to Israel in search of a better life.

The Israeli Law of Return allows all Jews to obtain citizenship for themselves and their spouses, children, and grandchildren. Thus around one million people from the Soviet Union came to Israel during the Russian aliyah, the big immigration wave of the 1990s. Among them were many non-Jews, whose mothers – just like mine – were not Jewish and who were therefore not considered Jews according to religious law. However, we were also non-Arabs and thus provided a suitable interim solution to the big demographic problem of the small Jewish state.

The newly arrived were automatically given Israeli citizenship. We naively interpreted the promise of equality that this procedure seemed to contain in the sense of 'we are all Israelis now', but this proved to be true only on paper. Again and again, we were confronted with the question, "Are you Jewish?" a query which made this one difference very clear. So when my grandmother died, my grandfather had to privately organize her funeral. As a non-Jew, she was not allowed to be buried in a 'normal' cemetery because the cemeteries in Israel belong exclusively to religious communities. In this and in some other life matters, such as marriage, for example, the State of Israel offers no support for its citizens who do not belong to any religious community.

As an Israeli teenager, I was desperately looking for belonging. When registering at school, the clerk told me that my great-grandfather's name sounded too Russian and that I might have problems at school. So I was given a better sounding name, which I carry to this very day. The symbolic shedding of the name and of the past made me feel that I can (and should) leave everything behind and start my life anew. I naively sympathized with Benjamin Netanyahu's first election campaign, whose book, *A Place under the Sun*, I swallowed almost in a single breath, as if I thought one could easily become at one with the nation by absorbing nationalist right-wing ideas. In order to be recognized as a true Israeli, I wanted to be a Zionist, an even better one than the Jews themselves. I still keep Ariel Sharon's autograph on a party flyer, as a reminder of that desperate patriotism.

Having been an Israeli for thirteen years, I still had the uneasy feeling of not being a real one. Furthermore, I felt I couldn't do anything to improve it. And since my homeland no longer existed in any meaningful sense, the only possible escape from that civil frustration was an escape forwards, or sidewards. I did not consider Germany as a serious alternative at first. I was indeed interested a little in that poetically square mechanicity of the German language, also a bit in philosophy, and in Krautrock and the music of two bands as different as Element of Crime and Einstürzende Neubauten. But there came a summer German language course that I spent at Freiburg University, followed a year later by an August at Humboldt University in Berlin and later, during the winter that immediately followed, a grant for a research project at the University of Duisburg-Essen. My stays in Israel became shorter, and I finally found myself registering at the Zehlendorf municipality in Berlin.

One winter, after I had spent the Christmas holidays with my girlfriend's family in Wroclaw, I took a train back to Berlin. I was in a good mood, felt strengthened mentally and physically by the family warmth that is traditionally accompanied in Poland by many a lush and festive meal, and I had with me a good book. I was also happy to be on my way back home. Yes, home – a home of my personal choice. Berlin was, at the time, still a little foreign to me, but all the more attractive for it. The main thing was that it was 'my city', declaredly so. There were still police controls at the German-Polish border back then. And when the German border police went through the train near Forst, I had to put aside my book – certain to have been one of Vladimir Nabokov's Russian-language novels of the Berlin period – and to show my Israeli passport. This unspectacular incident was accompanied by a strange and somewhat surprisingly strong and joyful feeling: to finally be home for real! Yes, right there on the train, not in a particular country with its specific language context, but right there – between countries and between languages. It was in that mobile Nowhere, that Inbetween, that I finally and paradoxically felt to have finally accomplished the task that in Israel felt so unattainable. I seemed to have finally arrived.

* * *

On the day of my naturalization, Ms. M. and I had more paperwork to deal with than usual – a signature here and a signature there, and here once again, please. But it was, at least on the face of it, a very usual office situation. And that's why that requirement came rather surprising. Ms. M. gave me an A4-sized sheet of paper, with visible signs of wear, and asked me to read "loud and clear" the large-print text on it.

"Just read it aloud?" I wasn't sure.

She nodded, and I read, "I solemnly declare that I will uphold the Constitution and the laws of the Federal Republic of Germany and refrain from anything that could harm it." I knew, of course, that at some point I would have to go through such a thing, but I expected to give such an oath in a more solemn situation – standing before a congregation, flowers here and there, among other somewhat embarrassed, smiling naturalization applicants, the faces from the poster with which Berlin promotes its naturalization programme. But being on my own with a clerk in her office, the situation immediately acquired an almost magical and somewhat creepy quality. If there is no audience to hear my oath, why does Ms. M. still insist on the ceremonial?

A breath of an invisible presence seemed to go through the room. I knew it – it was the presence of *Vater Staat* (Father State, the way Germans refer to their motherland). It was my first intimate encounter with him. So great was my confusion that I could not even apprehend the wording of that sombre commitment, let alone remember it later on. I Googled it, but finding it was not an easy thing to do. The Wikipedia article on naturalization did not help. I do not think I've ever seen a shorter page in the German Wikipedia.

Using the occasion, I also looked up the Soviet pioneer oath, which I also could no longer recall. There is only the memory of the anxious excitement when rehearsing it with my fifth grade classmates. Shortly after that, I remember having become sick but still happy to evade the actual ceremonial nervousness and pathos. They made me a pioneer anyway – without taking the oath, that is – possibly due to my good grades, but surely also because no one wanted to keep making a fuss about such petty business during the perestroika times. It was, after all, 1989.

* * *

Ubi bene, ibi patria. Having my first two patriotic efforts distorted by ideology, I can only adhere to Cicero's pragmatic view now. My country is there, where it is good for me. And how is it in Germany? Or, more precisely: How do I feel in your Berlin, thou Germany? I think I can now answer that in a calm, unexcited manner. My life as a new German will become a little easier, at least where bureaucracy is concerned. I am glad above all that I no longer have to spend time in the cheerless waiting rooms of the Foreigner's Registration Office in the Moabit industrial district of Berlin, which for a couple of years now I have been simply referring to as The Castle.

It was not only my passport that I used to hand over the counter to the obscure institutionalized caprice; emotionally, it was my entire future life. It was the feeling of being completely delivered, not being able to plan anything before they, behind their closed doors and unfriendly gazes, finally made a decision. Gradually though, I recognized that the prescribed response of the rigid bureaucratic machine to my organic life seems to be a challenge for the officials themselves. They were posed an equally unpleasant task of finding a more or less coherent and objective solution. Perhaps only by

OMNIUM GATHERUM

creating the conditions for this special type of insecure and difficult human solidarity does that institution become worthy of the Kafkaesque nickname I gave it.

I am German. Even though this simple and straightforward sentence still sounds quite strange to me, it is now a true sentence. With its first word I have a no problem. I know very well who is meant by the capital 'i'. The last word also seems clear. After all, I do come across quite a few Germans on a daily basis. Therefore, the problem that I still seem to have must be contained entirely within the verb 'to be'. I guess I'll have to wait and see what will become of that being.

DANIEL TKATCH has studied physics, art history, and philosophy in Israel, Germany, and Belgium and is now based in Brussels and Berlin. He is researching aesthetics and political philosophy at KU Leuven, and as a freelance journalist, he covers cross-national political issues and developments in visual arts from European and global perspectives.

THE KIDS KNOW WHY

Megan Beard

Arousing from the most profound of slumbers, we break the gossamer web of some dream.

Edgar Allen Poe

(For Chala.)

"What are they?" Paco asked, his voice high and cracking.

"They gotta be just quails," Tim said, lifting the bill of his Chiefs cap up, swiping at the perspiration that was collecting at his hairline.

"It's not quail season," Ally sneered. "Quail season isn't until fall. My dad and grandpa go out shooting then. It's too early."

Paco and I stood silently, not able to offer any additional words of wisdom.

"Screw this, I'll go look," Tim grumbled. He began to walk in the direction where we'd seen them. He was a husky boy with a yellowed T-shirt that read "I'd Fly 10,000 Miles To Smoke A Camel" with the image of a Middle Eastern man atop a dromedary zeroed in through the aperture of a gun. As he walked towards the grove, I remember thinking that his shirt was on backwards.

He gracelessly crashed through the brush, freezing in his tracks.

He began to scream like a newborn baby.

I can never remember if it's Robert Smith or the Pope who won't fly over Kansas, but I've heard both. It is only 27 miles from Lawrence to Topeka, but mentality-wise, it may as well be light years. Driving back to the old neighborhood where I grew up in Topeka, I thought of this. I always imagined myself eventually living in some far-off part of the world, like Paris or Shanghai, but instead I have settled only 27 miles away from the place I tried all my life to escape. I'm a Kansas girl, and blood is thicker than water. I'm a creature of habit and a homebody at heart. All the clichés you can imagine. After I graduated college, I kept right on working at my job as a secretary to a chiropractor, and I still work there now.

I came upon the "Welcome to Topeka: State Capitol" sign, and that old familiar gut-drop reared its head. No matter how welcoming that sign claims it to be, it will never feel welcome to me.

It was a bright, late September day. Indian summer, but fall did not dare show its face. It just kept right on being hot and muggy right straight through the season. Summer never really goes away in this state, it just takes a breather in order to rain down glassy ice cubes before it comes back again in a few months' time. The neighborhood block party reunion had been planned a year in advance. It's hard to plan outdoor activities in these parts, but September had seemed like a safe bet.

I turned onto Rochester Road, marveling that the old Piggly Wiggly where I'd worked throughout my teenage years was the same as always. It had been years since I'd been back to the old neighborhood. Once my mom remarried, our family had relocated to a nicer, newer, more anonymous neighborhood development on the other side of town. Even then, I'd still commuted across town to my old job. But I'd never dared venturing any farther than Walnut Lane. I stuck to the rules I'd set for myself once we'd moved out of the neighborhood. Easy to do if you're a creature of habit like myself, but today, those rules were going to be broken.

I sat at the four-way stop where Rochester is divided by Menninger

Road. The palms of my hands were sweaty and my heart pounding. Finally, I made the turn onto Menninger Road, instinctively slowing down as I passed the alleged stomping grounds of the Albino Woman: Rochester Cemetery. Local legend has it that she is the spirit of a mentally disturbed woman, whom people claim to see wandering around down by Shunganunga Creek, peering at them with bright red eyes. As kids, we'd always tried to contact her via Ouija board at slumber parties, and as teenagers we'd gathered down by the creek to smoke joints and see if the Albino Woman might care to join us. The closest we'd ever come to anything with glowing red eyes had been a rabid possum who'd charged at Paco, cornering him up a tree.

I veered right at the end of the road where Menninger meets up with the Kansas River, turning left onto Orchard Avenue. The trees were larger, but everything else remained the same. As I drove farther up the street, there were barricades blocking off the rest of the way. I parked my car nearest to them, grabbed my purse, and took a deep breath.

The classic rock station was blaring from across the lawns, where a massive boom box had been set up atop a card table. Mr. Patterson, Tim's dad, was manning it. Picnic tables had been set up along the sides of the streets, and the smell of grease and burgers wafted through the air. Of course Mr. Perez (Paco's dad) was in charge of the barbecue station. (It was his famed specialty; he had long boasted about his time perfecting the art of proper Kansas City barbecue during a stint at Fiorella's Jack Stack in Martin City.)

The old familiar faces were there, now aged and greying at the temples. Anonymous kids chased each other up and down the street, savoring the freedom of a car-free zone that allowed them to dart around higgeldy piggeldy. I felt as if I should know these kids, know their names and their family trees, but I felt as foreign as I did at the family reunions I so rarely attended, not quite sure who was who and who was related to whom. No matter how close I lived to these roots, my branches had been forever cut back.

I saw Tim, who was sitting on one of the picnic benches, a beer coaster nestling a tall boy. He was talking animatedly to a group of people around my own age. He'd grown into his huskiness and had fleshed out into a rather handsome grown man .

Our eyes made contact, and his smile fell slightly at the corners as dawning recognition crossed his face. I remembered a look similar to that when I was in high school. We had been sophomores at the time and were revolving through polar opposite spectrums of the teenage social hierarchy. I was one of the 'freaks', and he had been one of the 'preps'.

It had been during passing period. I was wearing black lipstick, a fishnet undershirt, and a Smiths T-shirt over it. He'd had on a white polo tucked into sedate khakis that still didn't hide his slightly duck footed gait (a defect that had never allowed him to be part of the football team). Despite this banishment, he was friends with all the prep boys – some on the team and some who merely hosted keggers and had parents with deep pockets. He was with them – a wall of boys with broad shoulders and intimidating gaits. A virtual Berlin Wall of Boys. Instinctively, my shoulders had hunkered into my torso, and I'd leaned my chin down as far as I could into my neck. Avoid eye-contact at all costs. As they'd walked by, crowding me up against the side of the lockers, he'd muttered, "Ugly bitch," and his friends rumbled in low guffaws.

"What is it Tim? What's the matter?" I called from where I stood on the hot pavement of Orchard Avenue's September street. He continued to wail like an infant, fanning his hands and slapping them in sickening circles, his wrists cracking. His face was bright red, but his lips were turning pale.

I gulped down my reluctance and proceeded forward. I smiled and

OMNIUM GATHERUM

made small talk with a few of the neighbors who instantly recognized me. An arthritic hand grasped my wrist, and I looked down to see Miss Henderson staring up at me through broad bifocals and her signature beehive.

"Now whatta you hafta say 'fer yerself, Erin Cook?" She smiled at me, broad white teeth curling back to reveal just the shiniest glimmer from the copper ridges of her dentures.

"Oh, not a whole lot Miss Henderson, how 'bout yourself?" I smiled down, giving her a hug. She had been a waitress as Bobo's Diner since 1963 and was a bit of a local legend. She had a salty personality that coated a ravishingly warm heart. Her favorite story to tell was that she'd been the girl who'd personally served a cheeseburger to James Taylor as he sat penning the song "Fire and Rain" in honor of a co-inmate he'd known while they'd been holed up at Menninger's Asylum for drug addiction. His friend had recently committed suicide.

"Just servin' burgers and pocketing pennies, honey," She shrugged indifferently, lighting yet another mentholated Virginia Slim. Oh, that familiar smell of Chanel Number 5 and menthol cigarettes! I'd spent many an afternoon hanging out at Miss Henderson's place, avoiding my parents' drunken fights, playing endless games of Old Maid with her on her sun porch in the summer time. I vividly remember her holding the cards up for close scrutiny, muttering with a skinny cigarette dangling from the side of her mouth, "They shoulda named this damn game after me," before thoroughly kicking my ass at the game.

After chatting with Miss Henderson, I made my way over to Mr. Perez's barbecue station.

"Hey Mr. Perez," I greeted him. A broad grin cut across his chubby face.

"Hey Erin! How you been doin'?" He scooted around the barbecue pit, enveloping me in a warm hug.

OMNIUM GATHERUM

"You know Paco's right over there," he pointed over to where Paco was sitting. Next to him was a girl with dyed black hair showing brown at the roots and a lip ring. She balanced a baby on her hip. Paco was covered in tattoos, but his signature blue mohawk had been shaved down to a more adult level than the great heights it had reached in school.

"Is that his baby?" I asked.

"Yup, sure is!" Mr. Perez grinned, "I'm a pappy! His name's Heath. Paco took it real hard when Heath Ledger died. You know how much he always loved Batman." I nodded meaningfully. We waved to each other, and I went over to where Paco was sitting with his girlfriend, Jenny. He also gave me a big hug, and Jenny's face lit up upon meeting me. I sat down next to Jenny cooing over Baby Heath, as Paco loped off to grab some fresh beers from the cooler. He plopped down next to me on the bench, handing me a bottle tucked safely into a Chiefs coozie.

"Yeah, got my own tattoo shop now. It's called Gotham City. It's out on Gage and Huntoon, not far from Jeremiah Bullfrog's. Those Homophobic Church Jack-Offs already picketed my shop 'cause we got a rainbow flag on the door, so business has gone way up! We're booked all the way through 'til November!"

"Congrats!" I laughed, clinking bottles with him.

"Have you seen Ally?" I asked him.

"Naw, she's down in Texas somewhere. I haven't seen Ally in years. Last I heard, she was all methed out."

"Oh shit," I muttered, taking a pull from my beer.

"Yeah," he nodded, "it's pretty sad." We both seemed to look up in the direction of where Tim was sitting at the exact same moment.

"Have you talked to Tim?" I asked.

"Pshaw. I got no reason to talk to that tool," he grimaced. "After everything he and his pack of douches put us through in school, why the hell bother?"

"Yeah, but," I paused searching for a way to broach the subject, "don't you ever think about that time... that time when we were ten... when we saw Them?" A dark cloud of comprehension crossed over Paco's face.

"I dream about it still," he finally said. "I... um... I get bad dreams. I, like, wake up sweating and shit. Like in a puddle of sweat. Sometimes I walk around. I – I'm on medication now... but it still happens from time to time. A few years ago, I started havin' what the doctors call 'Night Terrors'. I tore up a pillow... I woke up, and there was, like, white feathers floatin' everywhere. Then one night, it got so bad that I hit Jenny in my sleep... like really punched her." He looked like he was about to cry. Jenny ran her hand up and down his back.

"You didn't do it on purpose, hon. It was a dream. You had no idea what you were doing," she said patiently, obviously a subject that they'd talked about many times.

"Yeah, but I felt so horrible. It was so fucked up. I don't hit women," he shook his head. "That was when I got on them pills. Things've been better since then. Now I just sleep. It's all black, and I don't dream at all anymore." His words took on a hollow tone.

"I'm sorry I brought it up," I apologized. "It's just that... well, these last few years, I've been trying to come to terms with what we saw that day."

"It's better not to," Paco said. "It's better to stop thinking about it and just move on with life." We sat talking about less sensitive subjects, getting up periodically to help ourselves to Mr. Perez's smooth-as-butter baby-back ribs, tender skin dripping from the bone, and filling up on the micro-brewed beer that a friend of ours from high school was now bottling at his own little place out near Perry Lake.

All the beer quickly effected my thimble-sized bladder, and I spent a good deal of time going in and out of the Henderson's house to pee.

At first, I simply flitted through the house, all business, trying not to be intrusive. But after a few dozen beers and reminiscing about the old days, I stayed longer on my way back outside. I stood in the hallway studying the pictures on the wall. Little Tim in faded color photographs from the 80s became the husky, awkward, and sincere boy from my childhood. The boy who Paco, Ally, and I used to pal around with, built a tree house together with, tried our first cigarette (nicked from Miss Henderson's stockpile of mentholated Virginia Slim's, naturally) down by Shunganunga Creek with. A school picture from that year when we'd seen Them. The year that we stopped talking to one another, that year we were in middle school when social groups split us into factions based on our physical appearances and socio–economic brackets.

I slowly began walking to where Tim was standing.

"Erin!" Paco yelled. "Don't go! Stay here!"

"Shut up!" I hissed testily. I couldn't just leave Tim standing there like that. It was the same thing as when my parents had fights and they scared the hell out of my brothers and me. I always went downstairs to yell at them to stop yelling. You couldn't just let people carry on like that.

Tim stopped yelling, his arms falling helplessly to his side. His shoulders hung slack, like he was admitting defeat. I stopped in my tracks. I looked over my shoulder at Ally and Paco, who were standing with confused expressions on their faces. I shrugged at them, turning back to Tim.

"Tim? Are you okay?" I crept towards him, putting my hand gently on his shoulder. His face was stone, his eyes wide with fear. I followed along his direction of sight, gasping –

"Hey, Erin." I whirled around, my heart nearly exploding. Tim was standing in the hallway, his fists shoved into this pockets. He smiled bashfully.

OMNIUM GATHERUM

"It's nice of you to come out here," he nodded his head.

"Oh yeah," I ran a hand through my hair, trying to pull it together. "Well, it's been years since I came back here. Your house looks exactly the same."

"Yeah," he laughed. "Mom hasn't changed anything. Moms of only children get weird when they get older, so this place is like a Tim Shrine."

We laughed, and I leaned closer to him conspiratorially, "Actually, it always kind of was."

"Yeah," he giggled, "that's true." He looked down the hallway towards the front door, then turned back to face me. "Um, you know Erin, I was a real douche bag back in high school. Especially to you. You'd always been like a sister to me, and, um... what can I say? I was an asshole. I'm really sorry about the way I treated you."

"Yeah, you were a pretty big douche bag," I agreed, "but everything was different after we saw Them. Paco got all academic and into art, Ally got into drugs, you turned into some kind of big jock... I got... weird... er."

His eyes sparkled. "Them?" The color drained from his face.

They looked like quails. That was what I thought at first. That's what they'd looked like from a distance, anyway. A trail of quails walking one after another. Maybe a mother with her chicks. At first, it looked like they had feathers, but upon closer inspection it was revealed that they were covered in hair. It was matted, sort of a strange, mud-colored calico pelt with a whitish down that came up to the neck. Their legs were scaly, like bird legs, but they each had five knobby toes with jet black toenails corkscrewing out in bizarre angles.

They were walking out of a drainpipe that came out from the plot of vacant land beyond the yards. They were walking upright. Small people. They walked in a line. They were facing away from us, and I couldn't see their faces. But it was clear that they had no hair on their necks and heads. Their heads were bare, exposed and veiny like baby birds.

Tim's arms were outstretched, covered in bite marks. I grabbed his arm, pulling it close to examine. It was normal that he had those little red bumps, at least that's what I'd thought. He always got fed on by mosquitoes as if he was their own personal all-you-can-eat buffet. But, at closer inspection, I realized that they were like miniature teeth marks from miniature human beings. They bled in places. Tears were streaming down his cheeks. He was sobbing silently. I looked into his eyes, grasping his hand in mine. We watched as they walked from the cul-de-sac and across the hot pavement. I heard a gasp behind me and turned to see Paco and Ally standing behind us, watching this bizarre parade. Ally held her hands cupped over her mouth.

The small creatures walked in a single-file line, crossing through the pavement and onto Tim's yard. They marched towards the porch, then one by one disappeared through its white trellis. The last one turned around.

Its face was withered, like an old man's, but its eyes were blood red and sliced down the middle with a black sliver of pupil. It didn't have much in the way of a nose, just two small dots. Its mouth stretched around a row of slim, shiny barbed teeth, human-like, but filed down into little spikes. It made a sick little clicking noise, turning its head to the side as if it was trying to crack it, then sped up to ten times quicker than anything I'd ever seen and scurried into the darkness of the abyss below the porch.

Paco, Ally, and I stood dumbfounded. Tim slowly looked at us.

"They've never come out in the daytime before..."

He regained his composure, as if shaking off a bad fall. I wanted more than anything to have this moment with him, here, in his old house.

"Tim, for years I've thought about that day," I began. "I don't know when exactly, but at some point I started to think that I'd, like, dreamed it all or something. I've dreamed about it. I think Paco has too. But, you know, sometimes I think that maybe it was all just this weird collective hallucination... maybe they were just... I don't know... maybe they *were* quails."

Tim shrugged, a look of resignation on his face. He turned away from me, walking towards the door. It felt like we'd been having an argument about politics that had drifted over the line of tolerance into loathing. Maybe he still *was* an asshole.

"Erin," he called back to me.

"Yeah?" I narrowed my eyes, folding my arms across my stomach.

"It's hard for me to talk about Them. You only saw them once... but I lived with Them. I... I try not to think about Them anymore." He looked up at me, latching onto me with his eyes. "I just know that I'll never let my son sleep in this house ever... ever. Please. Let's not talk about this again." He turned and walked out the door and into the fading sunlight.

Megan Beard was born in Kansas City, Missouri on December 21st, 1979. She received her Bachelor of Fine Arts from the University of Kansas in 2003. After living in Chicago for several years, she settled in Brussels, where she currently lives with her partner and three cats.

THOU SHALT NOT SUFFER

_____

Embroidery by Megan Beard